Papago Park

POEMS

William Young

Acknowledgments

VERSIONS OF SOME poems in this book appeared in the following publications:

Agni, The Arkansas Review, Kentucky Poetry Review, Mid-American Review, Mudfish, Owen Wister Review, Sequoia, Shenandoah, South Ash Press, and *The Southern Review*

Contents

I

Sacajawea Sculpture, Cannon Beach

A woman and three men. You can
See right through them to the ocean.
Their bodies ocean. The wire mesh
Of their forms filled with the sea. A white gull
Flying, rising from Sacajawea's heart,
White waves breaking across her back.
Up close they smell of horses, the ocean.
Horses from Shohone kinsman.
Crossing Lolo Pass, followed closely
By David Thompson. British fur traders.
Missionaries, settlers, Mormons.

A sculpture is something to walk around,
Is time. From ocean side they're only
Asphalt and dwellings. Only black,
Shingled, a blue television playing
Inside their wire heads. Though now,
That I've sat with them these hours,
This squaw, these men, the straight light
Of the sky ignites them, yellow, then red.
Like human branding irons.
I walk around again.

Secret Passage Way

"I've never been up that way,"
She says, "where does it go?"
It's a blind alley, boxed in.
"To Whiting Street." "Oh."
She looks for a shortcut,
A literal one, or secret passage.
There's a hedge near the library
Just high enough to disappear
Behind. Of my town, too,
I remember not just
Spots of time but shortcuts
And paths, and in the woods
Cliffs and gullies, and vines
To cross over them.

We were not so much
Lovers of landscape as of
Places of surprise, arriving
Ahead of a friend, or suddenly
At the cemetery,
The new addition, or the Wabash,
The breeze in the swaying trees,
A sound like speaking,
And like our river. Wondering
How we ended up there.
Looking at each other.
But knowing the way home.

Recent and Forthcoming

Now you are a name, a contributor
I come across in magazines,
I read the bio's before the poems

To see what you've been up to, where you've been,
The way you want to be remembered,
And it's always Indiana, South Bend,

The Amish, those farm boy days in LaGrange.
Our first meeting in Vancouver you stood
Somnambulant as a horse on the Burrard Street Bridge.

Until the meal bucket came,
Until the lights came on in the bay as in a barn,
We swam from bar to bar, our lives the same.

Hoosier hysteria, high school marriages,
And of course the bread the Amish brought.
Heavy-bearded men, white-skullcapped women.

And driving out to buy tomatoes on River Road
(Or "tomaters," as my father said). The Wabash
Brown and soft as quills beyond the vegetable stand.

You planned your death at sea in imitation of Crane.
I was James Dean, a milk bottle to my forehead.
Intimacies grown strange,

A kind of grace, a kind of sorrow
Beneath snow-clouded mountains,
For a while there at the rim of the world.

But now you live in Santa Cruz,
In a house near the beach, among fields of artichokes,
Waves of green shadows.

The sea is pastel,
And the eucalyptus bend in the wind.
Everyone needs a Judas, you said.

Rio Salado, Tempe

They're working on the lake.
On the gravel bottom,
Clay is inlaid. The bridges
Are in place. The graded
Banks and the river or
"Lake" walk—it's been
Damned up for years—
Are finished. Now, at sunset,
Light glazes the tan clay
Vase-bright. And frat boys
Drunk on an evening walk
Are pitching beer bottles
From the lawn. Cars
Flashing by (lighting them
Like specimens in jars).
The bottom is filled with tires,
Boots, condoms, and song.
And army loiters here.
The most beautiful tomboy
I've ever seen, holds
Her camera by the lens
In her palm. The bottom
Is like the Wabash back home,
Polluted, gushy—the delicious
Ooze between the toes,
And wary of stepping on
A sharp rock or glass or catfish.

Marsden Hartley

He passed through Tucson
On the way to Mexico City.
The train, wandering among palms
And brick buildings
Welded, at sunset, land and him.
Later, at the hotel,
In the beautiful now restored lobby,
Across from the Moorish-style
Railway station, he rested,
The loneliest man on earth,
And lonelier than Edvard Munch.
There was one newspaper
And one radio station only,
Which created a certain charm,
A spell of sorts. So a blond boy
Passing along the sidewalk
Took him aback.

The names of his fate are Maine,
Cleveland, New York, Paris,
Berlin, Bermuda, and back
To New York, to Maine again—
A little island where boats
Gas up and get provisions.
Already in the rich dark acres
Of "Storm Clouds, Maine," 1906-7,
The rent of sky
Cuts a jagged insignia.
He lives now, as always,

Among a forest of boys.
A solitary boy kicks a soccer ball
Through the dark. The moon overhead
In the ink-blue night looks local.
His best work has begun.

Sunday, Nebraska

At the end of the field,
A swale by the tracks,
Rows curve
Against the grain,
A space opens,
The tractor's road home.

It's Sunday, no men
Or women around,
Corn stalks threshed
Snow level,
Light snow
Swirling, rising
Like a swarm of mosquitoes.
I ride through this
Small town and that,
The grasslands, the Black Hills
Going north
To the high dark of Canada.

Farmers emerge
From white church doors
Good News
Creasing their faces
Like an iron of God.
Two horses stand
At the railing, one
Spotted, one
Cinnamon brown.

Lunch in El Mirage

In the vacant lot next to the restaurant
The grass is yellow,
Broken bottles glint in the noon sun,
The houses across the way ramshackle.

But the cilantro is fresh, tangy, and the burro
Good. Little to do here but eat,
Drink, fuck, work on the car,
The occasional cockfight.

A Box of Nails

1

I saw my shadow today walking out
Before me. Bright, in detassled corn stalks
I saw the summer job I had: a boy,
My age, walking up and down the rows.
My second self, let's say, the acid trip or death.

A shadow runs astride the sidewalk, curves
Along the gutter, flicks through brown leaves.
I first remember light, so wintry, yellow,
My ears like iron burned and glowed at school.
The sky and land and town a monochrome.

Snowbank death, my body tingling
In the halls. Or sweating inside the gym
At basketball. Tomorrow, I've come halfway.
Something strange about my birthday falling
After Ground Hog Day. As if an after image
Emerged then, in a weak and weakening sun.

2

Mary Ann is reading Balzac on the couch.
She can read the same thing for hours. I sit
Typewriter-bound, revising fiction and stare
At townhouses—moon clouds above billowing
Threatening. Nothing is possible without
A woman back of me. Across the linoleum sky
Moves a long procession. Scared, I revise.

3
Sleepers in the park
Gather paper bags
And flagons and scatter
To the eaves of the library,
Running in thunder.

An Orthodox priest,
A raven, flies
Across Astor.
The sky
Like the Shroud of Turin.

4
I watched them sign. A flat hand rising near
The heart and shoulder twice, a smile–were they
Wishes of "Happy Birthday"? Or is it, "Strip."
One woman rouged and welted. All the while,
The yellow canaries gathering in the long grass meadow
And, in a single band, undulating in the wind.
The signers madly wave their hands.
"Crazy"–hand cupped to "c" before the eyes?
Heretics, Hawaiians, who knows. Old, I like
Television. But the pub fills, and I can't hear
Explanation. Good wine, sauvignon,
Swims in the tilted glass, red, opaque.
A finger from heaven touching the tongue. I wonder:
Tasty? Sex? A room full of gesturing drunks.
Then wings, air, the dumb show of the blessed.

5

Invertebrate snow, the storm at rest,
Fish-spines in the iron-gray trees.
The sun filters through stained glass.

Across the cold, blue-black asphalt,
A plow clears the major arteries.
A sweet motet betraying me.

Paradise. Long, Midwest
Afternoons. Sleds, rosaries,
Patrol guards, basketball, sex.

Under the canopy of this returning
Blizzard, the cadaver choir sings.
Empty rows rehearsing death.

In Winter and Summer

When she dips to unlace
Her white skates
Her corset falls away,
And panties float to the ice
Like butterflies.
Black, red, brown, and blond.

A Blackeye After Childbirth

At sunset in this bare land my daughter is born,
The sky Halloween orange, an autumn birth.
We couldn't be happier, two become three,
The wild-limbed labor spent in freedom.
My blackeye turning red, yellow, brown,
This last night before Sheri brings Mariel home.
And old Stones live album consuming
Extended adolescence in the milk-blue dawn.

Loosely interpreted, the background
Of screaming girls is a hurricane,
The skeletal chevron of Mick's teeth shines
In the arena. A sonnet of love increased by volume.

Octoberfest

He's a blessed one,
A mind as white as day. At night
Having forgiven again
All petty cruelty, all handsome torture,
His family is glad sees him coming.
They gather round and turn colors
Speak German (of trees) in a guttural wind.

The silver tops of earthenware steins
Glow, and faces curve
As in fun-house mirrors.
Deep in flora, arbor-deep,
He's forgotten the side he fought on.
He belongs to that autumn
Before the killing winter.

Leaving Wyoming

We were surprised
The cold passing in the night;
The vaunted storm heaving in the Rockies
Was gone come morning.
Only this beautiful tablet
Of snow left. You see,
We were too easily fooled,
Taken in by weathermen!
We slept through,
Barely nudging, barely dreaming,
Though the house like a cattlecar
Rattled through the dark.

But in the morning
The Chinook even melted the snow,
Sidewalks reappearing
Out of the night.
Trees rippling in aquatic BigSky
Our siren element.
My wife and daughter go off to school.
Light dapples the breakfast table.
Where I sit, beyond the storm watch,
Peaceful, in all my blood.

Noon at Bell Cemetery

My daughter likes to play
On the stones of the dead.
Here in the heavy graveyarded East–
Once more our summer odyssey.
Since our return I think
Mostly of ancestry and death,
This land of wood and stone,
Protestant and Iroquois.

It's clouded overhead, watercolor
Gray, the sun floating
Through the expanse
Like a blond spider.
Beyond the fence cows kneel,
Awaiting the rain. A land
Of light and shadow, x-rayish
As the ruby shade of beech trees.

An Idyll in Germany

His silvery shoulders shine
Like the white stones to the convent,
Their summer home in Nonenwerth.
Cosima, Christmas-born,
Watches Liszt bathe
In the waters of the Rhine.

Naked as daylight, ivory skin,
"Baptism by ice," he exclaims,
Enjoying as only the great can
Cold humiliation. And adds,
"If you're going to watch,
Daughter, at least scrub
My back." In Wagner's arms
She remembered her father in his youth.

Thirteen Ways of Looking at a Bed

"Our beds are crowded."
Freud

I
Among twenty golden dreams,
The bed
Was the only moving thing.

II
We three were in the bed,
Like a river
In which there are three branches.

III
The bed whirling in the dust storm
Was a small part of the movie.

IV
A man and a woman
Are one.
A man and a woman and a bed
Are one.

V
I do not know which to prefer,
The beauty of ripples on the bed

Or the receding light of the sun,
Sex
Or the afterglow?

VI
Leaves filled the windows
With ecstatic movements.
In bed he started
Reading The Boxcar Children.
He did not think he was
A reader as a kid
But this story came back to him.

VII
O thin men of Wall Street,
Why do you imagine
The chambers of kings?
Do you not see how a berth on a ship
Serves its purpose?

VIII
At Ikea they sell beds firm,
medium, and plush.
I'd never heard the last term.
But I know lucid dreams
And know, too, what
I've learned in bed is problematic.

IX
When the bed stopped creaking,
It signified the end
Of a round of sex.

X

The beds were covered with blood
In the green barracks.
And even the doctors expelled
Breaths and muffled cries.

XI

She converts almost anything
Into a bed. And suggested
They put the bed in the living room.
We're not expecting visitors, she said.
Once, a fear pierced him,
In that he mistook the shadows
Of the curtains for the bed.

XII

The sun is rising.
The child must be rising from bed.

XIII

It was evening all afternoon.
They dreamed
And were going to keep dreaming.
The bed sat in the corner
Of the bedroom.

Auden's Obsession

What suddenly brought so many to him?
Form or religion, some chord
Touched by his obsession–
Our turning away when someone else's
Daughter catches a foul ball
In the chest. For a moment horror,
Batter's guilt, but then
The last of the inning played, the infield
Smooth as a sand dollar's underside,
The breeze a soft eyelid on the lake.

However this time it was my suffering,
No turning, my daughter.
"I had a near-death experience,"
She said, only ten, the welt
An imprint of a rose on her barely formed
Breast, the nipple like a thorn.
We spent two hours in Urgent Care,
Everyone there, the receptionist,
The nurses, the physician, was a woman–
The doctor, visible through an opening,
Trimmed a boy's cut before sewing;
The overhead light was the face of an alien.

All the children sat in the waiting room.
Witness to our indifference,
Continually we fail to find
The air's door, and irregardless
Each day snap on the helmet of the sky.

The night, that night, slick as a polaroid,
We drove home through the shiny dark,
You were wanting your mother, my Ex.
Later, I lay in bed uneasily,
The tension about the shoulders
And neck like soldered wings.

Lizards

This landscape he always hated
And learned to appreciate
Is natural to his daughter.
The desert her home. "A lizard,"

She says, delighted—the tiny
Dinosaur pivoting
Its head, body stock still
Except for the pulsing belly.

She has seen lizards since three
Appearing in small crevices,
The pumiced ruins of their fence,
And shaded by tree, palms
That sway like lovers
Across each other.

* * *

She won't remember robins,
Nor winter, the plain quilt of land,
Dull-gold and dung-black fields.
Not the creek flashing through the trees,

Flashing across their faces
As they headed west, fording
The Missouri, past salmon-pink
Badlands, a father at the wheel,

Sky leaping from the horizon
Whirled from the axis.
At night, butterflies and
Grasshoppers meshed in the grill.
It will be lizards.
And a father who left.

Papago Park

We're lucky here, to be this far and inland,
The eye still miles away. No battening down
Or sandbags. Just far enough for rain and wind
To ripple desert palms, and shirts and gowns.
I drive this morning primed to admire hurricanes,
To sit at rest in softness, dying movements
As still it travels towards us near the plains.
But to my surprise I'm not alone. Adolescents
In cars arrive from every corner, walk
To large ramadas, silent, out of dark arroyos,
Are almost lemmings, zombies–do not talk.
Is it for school they come? Or some memorial?
Dust to dust. One gone too young. Or is it
To watch the hurricane brush the land so quietly?

II

Reading Irigaray at a
Coffee House

Isn't this also to be desired?
Suspended, a mere exchange among men?
No longer needing to be
Anything but abstraction. Just aorta,
Matrix, to be heavenly,
A mere transcendence.
No longer shit like Celia,
In circulation and as commodity
A kind of beauty, as when
A certain skin tone is like
Ice on the lake. Or walk
Down the runway, half naked
In boyish clothes, and realizing
Your existence preceded your appearance.
To bring light, holographic,
Happy to have no future,
Any past to speak of—

A representation of desires
You haven't any part in,
As pure as Helen,
Or the snow driven across Wisconsin
Any afternoon or this afternoon.
The light for an half hour or so
Around three, sometimes in winter
As late as four smacks
The red stop sign outside,

And the sign, now a shield
Sends light directly inside
Where, like a sea, it glitters,
Like an alien in a cornfield
No longer herself? To be
Easily translated, transported,
Isn't that a consummation
To be wished for? Yes. Still
One understands the other wish.

Promised Land

Here, you can't leer
At your neighbor,
As you see them
Everyday at their chores,
In slips and sandals,
Even if you're American.
What once was sex
Is sensuality or even
Less, a rhythm
Of sweeping and washing,
Hanging clothes,
Eating and sex.
Walking in the dust
To school in uniforms,
Going to the corner store
For load. No one
Sleeping in,
At least no women.
No transition
Either from sleep
To work, no hour
Of contemplation.
Just an endless
Filipino text,
Which itself
Has blended indecipherably
Into the rhythm
I've spoken of,
Word into flesh.

Guns

Another dark day in American history.
How incongruous and right slaughter
In Las Vegas. In France, they only
Have access to a knife, two young women,
Cousins, die in Marseille, victims
Of the madrasahs. Here 58 dead
And counting. Soon there will be
A moment of silence. For children
Gunned down in Newtown, for the parishioners
Gunned down, and on the streets of Chicago.
We'll turn to the heroism of the first
Responders, say nothing can defeat us,
We won't let this defeat us, when we are
United there is nothing that can defeat us.

Clear

In Cedar Rapids they hand sandbags,
In Germany he talks of bombing Iran.
The great tragedy is that he quit
Drinking and got clear, realized
His full potential, as a Texan.
The problem with the U.S. is Texas,
Or any President or CEO who
Fulfills the destiny of his, or her,
Home state, whether Hoosier, Buckeye,
Or Californian, who finally recalls
Everything, and vows now to get
The most out of life.

No longer living in a gated community,
So makes the whole world his stage,
Embracing every fucking thing alive,
As the levee breaks, as the feathery
Brown river exceeds its banks,
The local people starting to drown,
Their children logs floating down
Stream, toy houses in the flood.
You want to talk big, Lookie-Lou.
The children of Mohave Middle School
Are all egomaniacs.

One a brilliant poet (at least he kept
Drinking) and another a brilliant investor
(Who is a sex addict) thinking
Big and crushing local homeowners

In a brilliant agon. Give me those old
Fouled up guys. Not going to remake
The world in their image, not
So fucking twentieth century.
Who don't give a fig for the future.
Who watch the five-alarm fire

In Vacaville, the blue-white smoke,
And dream of semen and ice cream
And the sickness of family history,
And smile, a little self-satisfied,
But have in that rueful smile
The next election.

Brown Palace

After a while
He starts calling me "Billy."
I like this. I call him
Ralph Angel.

I meet an Irish woman
From Texas. She's never
"Felt Irish." We close
The place in the wee hours.

One fellow, Tennessean,
Is wry. And identifies a tv show,
Man with a Camera, apparently
No one but us ever saw.

The hotel itself beautiful.
Edwardian. Iron work like harp music.
The whole bit.
Brick Denver outside.

My brother arrived yesterday.
Two writing sisters
Are also here. We conferees
Waiting and drinking

(In that dull space between
A reading and the next meal)
At the Oxford near Union Station.
The art deco Cruise Room.

The Tennessean says:
"These curves, lines, and angles
Couldn't have happened
Before the twentieth century."

Zanplax

Some people experienced slight changes
In mood, attentiveness, sociability.
Some minor changes in temperature,
Sexual interest, or irritability.
Some bowel movements. Rash. Don't
Take Zanplax if you're currently on
Other medications, have high blood
Pressure, or are pregnant. Consult
A physician if you have any qualms
About adding Zanplax to your
Lifestyle. Don't mix Zanplax with
Alcohol or Mary Jane. Some people
Experienced euphoria, think there
Actually was a "Christ," or follow
New gurus who live in many houses.
Some, it's true, experience solidarity
And stop using Zanplax and move to
Wisconsin. But not a small minority
Of them commit suicide.
Did I say, Consult your doctor?
The people we have hired to read
Our commercials for Zanplax trained
At Juilliard. They are experienced
Shakespearean actors and suit the action
To the word. Which you don't always
Manage. Hardworking scientists gave
Their all to create Zanplax, which
Isn't available online or in the Philippines.
Go fuck yourself on Zanplax.

Stick Zanplax up your shoot.
Moloch of Zanplax. If your mother
Needs a lobotomy, like Francis Farmer
Did, I can only pity you. In Japan,
The cars are swimming.
In response to the tsunami.
We are sending ten tons of Zanplax.

I Am Curious, Blue

"I think it is a profoundly moral movie."
Norman Mailer

It is the boredom, the tedium of church
That constitutes its truthfulness. The ability
To represent the dull daily habits
Of marriage and children and abstinence,
Or whatever. Watch the three women
In their drab ankle-length winter coats
Walk through the blue snow—that a man
Who is saved goes to heaven, the Bible
Speaks of those...Yah. The way the men
Stand, folding one hand over another,
Loosely. I go to church each evening
And not for motorcycle killings.

And then I begin thinking about it,
Is the film shot in black and white?
All those close-ups of faces, on rippling
Water and saftig bodies, shadow
And light, as in Bergman penetrated
By cries, mourning, ducks on the lake.
Do the Swedes, even lesbian swedes,
Think of nothing else? The film silent
So only the hum of my VCR
And refrigerator limn the room
Where I watch this sequel, to Yellow.

* * *

"Soft, good, and warm." The old
European Sex/Politics theme,
Dated now in my livingroom. Even
The Swedish Negroes are not trustworthy.
For instance, Richard Wright.
"Come Lena." After a while
I simply transcribe action, muting
To keep up. Norman Dubie,
It was, who said he got
Most of his imagery from movies.
I thought, what an admission.
But his poems have a sensuousness
We only know from film.
Later, "firing the Surgeon General,"
The movie rewinds like a fishing reel.

Sky Harbor

A full moon, a Christmas star on the butte,
White columns of the Hayden Flour Mills.
Beneath the bridge, the rocks glisten, and
Its starting again, planes careening overhead,
Land tilted beneath the wing.
A scrabble board is thrust into the sky,
The collective unconscious buried in teeth,
Of the digital circuit of the city.
Bud Reed plays steel blues guitar,
And you hear the strum, the waves off Manoa,
The way she comes, the glasses on the bar
Like runway lights. O you, bombardier,

Mr. Huff, old formalist poet, chasing the sun
Through happy hour. Sails furrow the sea,
This Flanders Field of water; bones,
The color of semen, bleach the sand.
An ode to the Confederate dead
Now without history or depth, sun pulsing
Through charcoal depths, a jelly fish.
Do you hear the flag in the wind,
Its toy airplane sound? An air mask
Dangling like a piece of brain. The night
Like an unsealed envelope. You said
"No one knows who didn't fight the big one."

Then whispering: "I'll no longer be denied
Loveliness." We were so high up,
The big farm opening in the early dark.

Tina was at the register, her blouse lit up
Like a lampshade. Amputees flock
To the corner store and beg for change.
Waves spray pillars of the pier. Bodies float
Like poisoned fish. The palms bend
And float in the sky like seaweed.

I've been here before he thinks
And yet it never is quite the same.

Spawn

After all, not
one of the Originals.
After the toil, one
Who stands in shadows,
The shadow moving across
My face like something
From *Dorian Grey,* when
All the while I wanted
To be someone in
Happy Hollow with the other
Boys showing our peepees,
Coming across arrowheads,
Small and sharp, gray
And black or white,
Offering instead commentary,
But at the service
Of a diminishing Republic
Having recast my
Article, not bullfighting,
Witness to the breakdown
Of the narrator,
But not allowed one
Myself, not even anymore
Those terrible images
Of salmon, blindly
Fighting their way upstream,
Slapping against the waves,
The terrible word "spawn"
An only inheritance.

Bad People

For a while it was this:
People were frustrated, ignorant,
Neurotic and self-concerned.
It was best to give the benefit
Of the doubt; it was in one's
Best interest to do so.

But listen to that language, its
Unfuckableness, its
Weakness, like the afternoon sun
At dusk, but not even as strong
As that. These people, I tell you
Are evil. There are very evil
People all around you.

In the halls of academe, in business
Corridors, in hair salons, car
Dealerships—you name it—
There are real evil people
Who lives next door, take out
Their garbage, invite your child
Over for a swim, close their windows
At night and watch television.

You don't believe me? Listen,
These people are evil. Not
Merely professional. Not only sick
But evil. I'm telling the truth here.

Don't trust these people. They're
Hell's people. They're killing the earth.
Some of them wear short pants
Like mailmen. Believe me,
These people are bad.

Literary History

We found a journal
And created a movement.
Of course there are
Fine poets who are not
Part of the movement
But they are not
Part of the movement.
We're having the time
Of our lives. You
Should be at our
Drunken parties or
Create your own.
We thought of it
Before you did and
Are having a hell
Of a time. But the
Happy thought is
You can do the same
Just choose something
To concentrate your
Energies on. Kerouac
And Ginsberg changed
History. And just
Think of the wild
Time they had. I'm
Already nostalgic for
Our movement even though

It's scarcely begun.
Our journal is popular
Without being multi-
Cultural. Our
Parties are the best.

Becoming Another Person, And Hearing Different Melodies

From this day I'll live like a King,
I mean live cruelly.
I've everything of a King,
Except noble birth and riches.
But the word rolls off my tongue
Like heads across the palace steps,
"King," not prophet or poet.
One who matters, like food, sleep,
The breath of foreign ladies. Such grand
Persistent dreams. From this day
Unfair as weather, incontinent as spring,
Ancient as the millionth winter!

The palace is only too full
Of those seeking arbitration.
Breakfast in bed will not
Be so much once I learn
Obedience to who I am
And something of the grander manner.
From this day forward, acceptance
Of divine order and
The rose's bud. Never giving in
To the language of the ox-cart owner.
Never, never. Always that
Song of another kingdom.
Such ignorance, I put to death.

The Death of Monsieur Royal Of the Cirque du Soleil of Montreal

I'm led in an indigo door
And out the same again. Another
Man's reserved seat is up
The rope ladder near the swinging
Trapeze. Your white linen suit
Monsieur Royal, shifts easily as you move.
Your cockeyed hat also moves.
It's French, light, absurd. Through the door
Come Gina and Balthazar, red clowns, in suits
Too large. One thing and then another.
They won't listen to you and swing
Buckets of confetti up
Into the audience. Cutting up
As usual. But you, Monsieur, moved
Quickly to stop them, your coattails swinging.

French pastels color the doors,
Blues turned to pinkish tints. Another
Act enters, in skimpy suits.
Those bad clowns again. Their suits
Bring a gasp: Balthazar's codpiece up;
Gina in sequins. It is like no other
This circus. Small, medieval. You move
Forward to announce the acrobats at the door,
As trapeze artists fly above, swinging
With grace and timing, in resplendent suits.
Through the lilac-colored trap door
You disappear, as they swing high and higher up.

In your absence Balthazar and Gina movingly
Enter the arena. Gina sulks; her other,
Worse half trying to make up. Another
Act, the acrobats, swing
Each other. The contortionist moves

Forward on his elbows. His strong suit.
Applause. The crowd standing up.
A genial chaos reigns, but a door
Reveals the movement of two clowns unsuitably
At each other, doggie style. Fed up,
You swing round, and withdraw through a different door.

A Poem

Where do we see each other, where
Shall we meet, if not at Opera-Comique,
Or Buffa? Where from afar

May I admire you and your husband
Despise, or your current lover, when
There's no central locations, no

Prescribed social order, nowhere less
The riff raff (except for the journalists)?
Ah for a pair of opera glasses!

Perhaps in Hollywood there are places
Where across a blue pool one can
Watch and be watched in the manner

Befitting my desire as you move
In the arms of another, your arms bare
To the shoulder, your smile dead as water.

But no Fitzgerald revival will bring to me
That world. No one will write a novel
Or play about us, and our suffering reward.

Comus

His copy of *Moby Dick*
(Which mostly I read)
Was ruined in a flood
In of all places Arizona.
I'd never read "Comus,"
So take the book along
With me on a walk.
Standard English Classics,
Copyright 1900.
The introduction is by
Tuley Francis Huntington
(A.M., Harvard),
Instructor in English
In the Leland Stanford
Junior University, sometime
Head of the Department of English
In the Southside High School
In Milwaukee.

My grandfather, too,
Started as a high school
English teacher before taking
His A.M. at Columbia.
I'm a little worried
About damaging the book
Which I've got
In my back pocket.
I liked "L'Allegro" and
"Il Penseroso" in college,

But dropped out of Milton
When we came
To *Paradise Lost.*
It was a scorching Phoenix
Summer. I stayed inside,
watched Watergate, and drank.

Grandpa's marginalia is in pencil.
This morning something
Rather strange happened.
I went to print out Stafford's
"Traveling through the Dark"
And, when looking at criticism,
Saw my name there.
"Young suggests the [car]
'Purrs' and seems to make
Its own decisions to swerve."
It was funny to see my name
So second-hand. Never
Had I a literary conversation
With my grandpa—he died
When I was sixteen of throat cancer.
I remember him coming
Half-way down the stairs,
In a purple robe, his hand
On the railing, to say hello.
"He's been so brave,"
My grandmother said.
(I hadn't wanted to visit
Because I would miss
The Christmas basketball tourney).

* * *

His notes, handwritten
In the back of the text,
Describe a masque as a play
Held at special occasions
In Courts and Palaces—
Best actors of the time
By best families. Originally
A danse by masqued figures.
Always a dance of monsters
And one by refined people.
Allusions of great persons.
And a pastoral element.
Milton added dialogue
And plot, if not conflict.

They were all Christians—
My father, too—
Though I am not,
And so wonder what
My grandfather had to say
About Comus.
Grandma said,
This even before I got
My high school girlfriend
Pregnant, that there's
No such thing as free sex.
I dropped Milton
But took Shakespeare
From the same professor.
Dr. Evans. I think
Of him, too. Of
Critics and men.

III

Early to Rise

The double doors that lead
Out of my bedroom are made
Of maplewood, wood strips
Sectioning off glazed glass.
The morning sun rises behind
Like an aura. Such mornings
I'm convinced of a holy presence.

The sun lights up the snowflaked
Glass, and the wood strippings
Appear like a row of crosses
On the morning of the Ascension.
I have not gone to work.
The day appears to offer
More than labor and routine.

The sun spreads across
The glass as though on water.
Perhaps the cold lust will be
Shaken from me, like winter,
And liquor will cease to be
The great transformer.
It is too early to tell.

And So The Prayer Is Offered

I have no plans to get drunk.
But to sip the day away,
Translating from the original.

At Forty-Seven

My third life
Closes quietly.
No celebration.
Even my daughter
Had other things on.

But I'm alright
With it. A staircase
Of sunlight
Inaugurates
A fourth one.

Round Tunnel

The light is like a tooth
At the end of the tunnel.

The light a penguin
At the end of the tunnel.

The light is a lot like a hat
At the end of the tunnel.

The light is like a flame
At the end of the tunnel

Blinding going out of the light
And going into the light.

The light is melancholy
At the end of the tunnel.

Like shoulders of a woman
Or a man. Like sand.

The light flows toward us
And away from us.

The light is like a stone
At the end of the tunnel.

Signs

When the signs were vertical,
Like the old C
           L
           E
           A
           N
           E
           R
           S
                  sign,
Where you follow the letters down,
The world was better.

I'd settle for a red and yellow
SHELL.

Now the signs are horizontal,
Plastered on the front of a building
Or blazoned across your path
Even the fonts unsingular. Egregious
Ones like AUTOZONE.

Virility

She loves nothing
So much as to see
Her man go off
To work, to his job,
The only kingdom
She understands
Him in. At home

Headbent before
The television or at
The supper table,
Silent as the snow,
He is everything
She dreaded in her own
Father, his long
Decline. At daybreak

She's happy as she
Will be the entire
Day. She follows
To her own job,
But still likes to see him
Go out first,
Turning to wave,
Crossing the snow
Into the sunlight.

Apartment

I've been in this apartment a year
On the second-story overlooking the city.
All along I was reminded of an apartment
I had in Boston and of my brother's

In San Francisco. The windows raise up
Instead of sliding the modern way.
The wainscoting is old and lovely.
There are two built-in bookshelves.

But this morning—perhaps it was
The gray light or something else—
I realized this place is like the one we had
In Canada when we were young
Graduate students and you went crazy.

Single Outlet

I pull on the cord
To the clock to plug
In my typewriter.
Time stops, though
The music of Bach
Plays on attached
To the other half
Of the socket.

I rest a few bars.
My Smith-Corona
Hums in the background,
Belt-driven,
The sound like an
Erector-set motor.
The grinning keys
The grill of a Buick.

Dark falls, and I
Must choose: light
Or music. Do I
Know these keys
Well enough to play
By touch? No.
Someday my fingers
Will cramp in this
Praying mantis pose.

* * *

So the music must
Stop. I rattle on
Without time
Or melody. Only
This bare fixture
Above me, its
Unmediated light,
Naked as the
Alphabet below.

Darkest Evening of the Year

Since I don't have to teach,
I arrive at the final drunk,
And quote a line from Frost:
"Soon it will be pitch dark."

For even if it's only noon,
And rain not snow, the desks
Are in a row, and it's dark
Beyond belief already.

School Nights

Although these days it's not
Unusual for me to be heading
Home when others, mostly young,
Are just starting their evening,
It seemed tonight the bookstore
Was especially filling up just as
I was about to leave, until I realized
That it was Friday night and thus,
Except for me since I taught
A Saturday class, the weekend.

And so, for them, the beginning
Of leisure, of the pleasures of books,
Coffee, and company, and later drink,
Tv, movies, or sex. But for me,
The remembrances of school nights.

Womb

And then as dark falls at the hotel
And the atrium is floodlit,
And the sliding doors of the rooms
Facing a brain-dead drop to the lobby
Begin to come on,
And the small clatter of dishes, chatter,
And the sound of waterfalls registers,
I understand this solitude I live in
Has a kind of spaciousness.

The tall black man sits down
Again at the piano,
His hand fluttering
Like a white moth on the porch.
The village blazes.
Everyone seeks a new dwelling.

Antiquity

Fifty-five feels like a watershed.
In ways even fifty didn't. Perhaps
It's just the accumulation of other
Watersheds, other losses. I haven't
Lost anything recently, I'm just
In a different place. The air
Breathes on me, but not with hot
Breath but as if a fine light,
And the world rebounds at my feet
And I lean in like a wrestler
Who stands naked and muscular
On an antique vase, ready
To erase 2000 years of nonsense.

Architecture

1

The entrance runs parallel to the center of worship.
One arrives as if from an inside to an outside,
Almost a kind of park or picnic area
In which workers, some solitary, some in twos
Or threes, or families, have come at noon.
The stone looks like wood, balsa or ply,
On a huge scale, blond and fitted–intimate–
Like something I might have planed myself in shop.
Even if I don't genuflect before sitting in the pew
And merely watch those at prayer hands folded
Or fingers splayed before their eyes, I feel
Drawn here today and feel something new
In the architecture. The Christ is lithe as Donatello's
David, bronze against the pale white-yellow cross.
I walk the length, from font to apse, past all
The Stations of the Cross, past lithographs
Of many saints. The victims of child abuse,
Whose eyes I didn't meet when entering,
Are still outside. Leaving, I see a woman drive by
And cross herself as she passes the church.

2

The winged thing across the way
Is Gehry's latest. The Disney Concert Hall.
It's more like waves I guess,
If waves were aerodynamic. This day
It's as gray as the wintry sky, the waves
Of sheeted metal carving the space.

I like it, too, and walk across
The construction site to stand near to it
And feel the pleasure as in the church
Of being outdoors, or near nature.
I'm only downtown for jury duty, as
We twelve decide if Mr. Beasley
Deserves an extra million in severance pay.
He's white, young, seems nice enough.
Someone loves him. Mr. Beasley's money
Is our focus for unlimited days.
The courthouse is a marble mausoleum,
Even cell phones don't work. Tomorrow,
We're released for Good Friday services.

3

Which I attend. My jury service—my first—
Causing me to become newly born
To the lives of others, from Mr. Beasley
To the judge on the bench, to the clerk and court reporter,
To the many walks of life represented among us.
The difficulty in life is to learn to stand
Eye to eye, to stand equal to all, neither up
Nor down, a man, a person among others, in nature.
To stand eye-to-eye level even with the giants of antiquity,
A Shakespeare or Jesus. The entrance
To The Cathedral of Our Lady of Angels is, as I said,
Indirect, down a long swale which resembles
A tunnel and leads to the rear of the sanctuary,
Past the ancient retablo, rose and gold,
The gilding in final stages of loss of compensation.
And the place still half-empty, one can't but hope
The Communion Service—the plot—might somehow be delayed
Or forsaken, so we might simply exist in the architecture.

Although what's not to like—the glorious pipes rise vertical
And blow out perpendicular low rumbling tones
As we await the packed house. And interestingly,
In light of my service, new notions of truth are arrived at:
Yes, Jesus fulfilled the scripture by his crucifixion.
An eye witness account tells of the blood
And water which spread from his side. But the Cross
For Christ was not the end, crucifixion
Not the last chapter. Forms of petition and prayer
Continue, as well as our hymns.

Moths

When I open the door the moth
Moves out of the floodlight.
How long since I've seen
A moth, and how I feared them
Back in Indiana beating against
The yellow light, butterflies night twins. ·

How easily both lose their skin
Coloring we were taught. And how
I remember my brother's
Collection for Freshman Biology,
The butterflies, moths, and beatles
Under the glass case pinned.

The brown or gray moths were far
Scarier than even the worst
Insects, even ones with claws.
Moths like something never fully
Exposed, of old stone porches,
Negatives in a dark room.

Lovers

Even now it seems a lovely delusion.
"I once read Miles Davis autobiography,"
He says, to his girlfriend who listens,
As if he is part of the jazz world
And we all are. And perhaps it's
Not delusion, but just indulgence,
Lovely as youth spent in North Beach
Or Venice, in washed-out clothes,
Reading the classics, old and new,
Fucking shyly, tenderly to the sounds
Of Bill Evans, knowing for the first time
In your life Black friends, having
A vegetarian diet, a Shepherd who goes
Everywhere, and hurt feelings
So astonishing you carry them low.

Last Days

He says to tell them
Their wedding present
Has been sitting on a shelf
For three years
(Closer to five, I bet),
But they'll have to
Come to St. Louis
To get it because
It's too fragile
To send. Besides,
It's been there
For so long
They've come to
Think of it
As their own.

for Brian

'O My Soul

My soul left my body
Ahead of my death.
But I look out now
At the world with
New attention.
Listen to the wind.
Emptied. A place saver
For the next generation.

"Smoke"

I'm thinking I don't remember
(Or recall) this Larkin poem.
It must have been written early on
Or discovered among his papers.
It's rather thrilling to see him
Write about a city–"vanishing before noon/
or was it earlier?" I glance at the stanzas:
"She'd come on Friday after work
all the way/ from Toledo
and he'd dressed in his only suit."
Wondering is there a Toledo
In England? And then he mentions
Friends: "Bernie, Stash, Williams,
and I." Even though he didn't marry
Larkin did have many friends,
Hilarious are his letters. I shut the book
Astonished, thinking that I'll read
The poem more closely later. And once
The kids have gone to bed
And I've turned on the fan, I do.
Philip Levine, it says. Someone
In fact I briefly knew years back
At a writers' conference.

April 9, 2018

Perhaps I should brush away
Debris and dirt, the small desert rocks
I associate with Arizona,
The letters in relief,
"Brian Robinson Young,
1959-2014" (remembering admirers
Left beer bottles for Kerouac).
I just sit down on the bench.
It's early but already the heat
Is rising, my armpits damp,
The two-toned mourning doves,
Warblers, and another bird's
Chugging sound notes in the xeriscape.

What Mom refers to as
The most beautiful tree,
Palo Verde, have bursts
Now of yellow while
Brian's tree hasn't
Grown much and still needs
Posts and wires to hold it up.
The bougainvillea is deeply pink.
The underside of a hummingbird
Flashes like dice, the rocks purple, and
The boulders, shades of sand,
White, and bronze, are like
Misshapen growths and emblematic.

* * *

He ruefully referred to himself as
A twentieth century person,
Nature the great innovation
In modern art and poetry,
Going outside the big change,
The two of them traveling
And camping, with a pioneering spirit.
I sat with Mom who lost a renegade son.
At the memorial, Jenny
Told the story of Brian dreaming
Of diving down in the water
To save the family, and of her
Then diving down to save him.

Like a Zion Psalm

The clouds move overhead,
Powdery orange, and the gulls
In loose formation
Are quiet for a change,
Crossing the expanse.

But I sit in my car
Readying for the day.

www.ingramcontent.com/pod-product-compliance
Lightning Source LLC
LaVergne TN
LVHW041202080426
835511LV00006B/712